Top Hat Tompkins, The Detective

by Jason Lublinski

illustrated by
Aleksey Ivanov

Scott Foresman
is an imprint of

Glenview, Illinois • Boston, Massachusetts • Chandler, Arizona
Upper Saddle River, New Jersey

ISBN 13: 978-0-328-51670-4
ISBN 10:   0-328-51670-8

10 11 12 13 V0FL 17 16 15 14

Top Hat Tompkins was the youngest detective in the entire world.

Although he was very young, he was also very famous. Important adult detectives from faraway countries like Germany and Peru often came to visit him and ask for help. They came from far and near because Top Hat was such a great detective. He could find any missing person or item, no matter how lost it was. He could solve any mystery, no matter how mysterious it was.

Wherever he went, Top Hat always wore an enormous top hat. He believed that a detective should dress well and felt that a top hat was the nicest of all hats.

One bright, sunny, spring morning, Top Hat was working in his office when his good friend Sid Sefferlump ran into the room.

"Salamanders!" Sid exclaimed.

"What was that?" Top Hat asked.

"Salamanders!" squealed Sid again, this time a bit louder. "Oh! Ooh! SALAMANDERS!!!"

"Sid, you're my very best friend," said Top Hat patiently. "But I have no idea what you're talking about. Try saying something other than 'salamanders.'"

"I . . . that is . . . my . . . my salamanders are missing!" declared Sid.

"Missing?" asked Top Hat, surprised.

"That's right!" said Sid. He was having an easier time talking now. "They're missing! All seven of them!"

"That's terrible!" said Top Hat. He knew just how important Sid's salamanders were to him. Ever since Sid had first learned about amphibians from reference books and a zoo exhibit two months ago, he had fallen in love with the little creatures.

"So, what happened?" Top Hat asked his friend.

"Well," Sid began tearfully, "I was at Hennessy Park, playing 'King Arthur' with my salamanders on a picnic table. I'd just put the salamanders into my model fort, when I saw a bright yellow butterfly fly by.

"It was so pretty that I decided to follow it," he continued. "When I got back to the picnic table, the fort was gone! And so were my salamanders!"

"All that was left was a big puddle," Sid sniffed.

"A puddle?" asked Top Hat. "How mysterious!"

"You're the greatest detective in the entire world, Top Hat," said Sid. "Can you help me get my salamanders back?"

"Sid, I'd be happy to help," said Top Hat. "Was anyone else at the park when they disappeared?"

"Yes," replied Sid. "Penny Prundle, Ralph Moobly, and my older brother, Hugh, were all there. Do you think one of them took my salamanders?"

"Could be," said Top Hat. "Let's go investigate."

A few minutes later, Top Hat and Sid arrived at Penny Prundle's house. They found her reading a book.

Penny was the prettiest girl in the neighborhood and one of the smartest. Top Hat didn't think she would be cruel enough to take Sid's salamanders. But as a detective, he also knew that you could never be certain about these things when you were dealing with crime.

"Hello, Top Hat," said Penny. "Hello, Sid. What are you doing here?"

"We've come to ask you a few questions, Miss Prundle," replied Top Hat. "Exactly what were you doing earlier this morning? Around ten o'clock?"

"Why, I was at the park," said Penny. "I was practicing a song."

Penny began to sing. "Twinkle, twinkle, little car. How I want to drive you far!"

"Aha!" shouted Top Hat. "Very interesting! Thank you for your time."

As they left Penny's house, Sid asked, "Did you learn something important, Top Hat?"

"Oh yes," said the detective. "Penny said she was singing 'Twinkle, twinkle, little car. How I want to drive you far!' But everyone knows that the words are 'Twinkle, twinkle, little star. How I wonder what you are!'"

"Does that mean that she stole my salamanders?" asked Sid.

"It may," said Top Hat. "Or it may simply mean that she does not know the right words to the song. We won't know until we talk to Ralph Moobly."

A few minutes later Top Hat and Sid were talking to Ralph Moobly, a short boy who always wore big, dark sunglasses.

"This morning? Well, uh . . . I was working on my slap shot," said Ralph, looking uncomfortable.

"What do you know about salamanders?" Top Hat asked him.

"Eughh!" replied Ralph. "I don't like lizards. Nasty, scaly little things! Reptiles! Bleahh!"

"You take that back!" shouted Sid.

"Calm down, Sid," said Top Hat hastily.

Top Hat and Sid walked away from Ralph, who went back to playing street hockey.

"So, what did we learn?" Sid asked excitedly.

"Well," said Top Hat, "Ralph made an important mistake. He called salamanders reptiles, but they are amphibians. That means that they spend part of their lives living in the water and part on dry land. Also, Ralph called them scaly. Everyone knows that salamanders do not have scales."

"I know that Ralph was wrong. But does that mean that Ralph took my salamanders?" asked Sid.

"Perhaps," said Top Hat thoughtfully. "Or perhaps it simply means that he does not know much about salamanders. We will have to talk to your older brother, Hugh, before we know for sure."

They found Hugh in his bedroom, which was freezing. It was freezing because most of the room was a giant, walk-in freezer. Hugh was standing inside it, happily making ice sculptures.

"Oh," Hugh said to his brother, sneering. "I see you brought along your friend, the world's greatest detective."

"Hello, Hugh," said Top Hat, ignoring the older boy's sarcasm. "We wanted to ask you a few questions. What were you doing at ten o'clock this morning?"

"Well, that's easy," Hugh replied. "I was at the park. I was reading a book about Sir Edmund Hillary. He was the famous explorer who traveled to Antarctica."

"You really like the cold a lot, don't you?" asked Top Hat.

"You've got that right," said Hugh. "I LOVE the cold. You see all these beauties?"

He pointed to a series of ice sculptures arranged around his walk-in freezer. They included an ice castle, an ice swan, and a birthday cake made out of ice.

"I made them all myself," said Hugh proudly.

As soon as Top Hat and Sid went back outside, Top Hat turned to his friend.

"I have one last question," he said. "But this time, the question is for you. The fort you were using to play King Arthur . . . did your brother make it for you?"

"He sure did," Sid replied.

"Just as I thought," replied Top Hat. "Sid, give me ten minutes. I think I will be able to recover your salamanders for you."

"Really?" asked Sid excitedly.

"Yes, indeed," said Top Hat. He set out at a
fast walk. Sure enough, ten minutes later he was
back, holding the seven salamanders in a small
plastic box.

"My salamanders!" shrieked Sid. "They're
back!"

"They were easy to find, once I knew where
to look," said Top Hat with a smile. "Can you
guess?"

"No!" declared Sid. "I'm stumped! I'm baffled!
I have no idea whatsoever! How did you do it?"

"Everything made sense once I learned that your brother likes to make things out of ice," replied Top Hat, still smiling. "When you told me that he made your fort for you, I guessed that he had made it out of ice too. You see, Sid, nobody stole your fort or your salamanders."

"Really? Nobody?" asked Sid, confused.

"No," said Top Hat. "You see, water changes its form at different temperatures. If it is cold enough, water turns to ice. If it is warm enough, that ice starts to melt. And today has been a very warm, sunny day."

"You're saying my fort melted?" asked Sid.

"That's right," said Top Hat. "When the fort turned to water, it left a big puddle behind. I found your salamanders wandering around in the tall grass beneath the table."

"Why didn't I remember that ice melts in the hot sun?" complained Sid.

Just then, a tall, red-faced boy came running up to them.

"Top Hat!" he bellowed. "You have to help me! Someone has just stolen my rare and priceless snowman collection from my backyard!"

"Oh, dear," said Top Hat.

Water's Many Forms

Water can take many forms depending on its temperature. It can appear as a liquid. It can also turn into a gas or a solid!

If you heat water to 212°F or higher, it boils and turns into steam. Steam is a gas.

If water cools to lower than 32°F, it freezes. It then turns into its solid form, or ice.

If the temperature is higher than 32°F, ice begins to melt. It turns back into its liquid form.